WORDS
WITH
STEVE
JOBS

ALSO BY BRIAN BARTON

WORDS
WITH
STEVE
JOBS
BRIAN
BARTON

Words with Steve Jobs is a registered trademark.

ISBN-13: 978-1535101233
ISBN-10: 1535101237

This is a work of creative nonfiction. It is not reportage.
All steps have been taken to ensure that every aspect of
this story is true. However, it may contain errors and/or
omissions. Any misrepresentations are unintentional.

For J.Y. and D.M.T.

"N_{o.}"

So began the personal email I received on May 2 from Apple CEO Steve Jobs.

I remember the date because of the incident. The scrap. The dustup. My dog and I had gotten into it at the café.

It was one of those impossibly nice Fort Greene mornings. Calm. Not humid. Temperate, but not cool. I'd awoken early and found the park quiet.

Maintenance workers had come and gone, leaving only damp footpaths and lawns edged to perfection. The day seemed filled with promise.

Shadow and I nosed around the park's perimeter. She sniffed the ground while I looked up at the oaks and maples towering overhead like giant corn stalks, leafy with greens and golds. And there was more good news: My Black Labrador had done her business shortly after our arrival—in a quantity that matched the size of my plastic scoop.

I doubted the world could hold more magic, but all that changed at the café.

I was ready to leave as soon as I got there. Drinking my latte indoors was killing me precisely because it was so nice out, but the benches outside were packed so I was stuck inside on a stool. And I was as steamed as my milk. I was halfway out the door with my coffee and laptop when I saw a couple vacating their spot outdoors.

Shadow stood up as I walked outside. She inched in my direction, her tether rubbing against the tree where I had leashed her. Her whimper was in the air, but I kept walking. I mean, I could have untied her, but I wanted to work. She resigned herself to the ground and sighed.

And then I saw her face.

She had this forlorn look in her eyes, like a Gitmo detainee or a five-year-old pining for dessert. Her soft brown eyes caught mine and I kinda lost it. *My baby*, I thought. I walked over, untied the leash, and set my latte on the ground.

"Good girl, Shadow!" I said, crouching down to her level. I undid the lead and leaned in for a kiss. She bounded toward me, then faked right for the cup of Italian roast.

Fuck! That's my coffee, you mangy mutt! is what any sane person would've said. But I was morning-impaired and slow to react. It was like accidentally dropping a dish. There's always that quarter-second of recognition where you watch it falling and think to yourself: *Shit, I just broke that.* You see it happening and yet you can't do anything about it.

Like that.

She nosed into my coffee and lapped up a full swig. My body didn't respond until I saw that pink tongue dart into the cup, but once I did, I yanked hard on the leash. She skidded back toward me with the sound of toenails scraping on concrete. I'd gained the upper hand. And now I tightened my grip.

That'll teach you, I said to myself.

Her muzzle neared me and I noticed it was covered in white and brown powder. *Strange,* I thought. And then I remembered the generous dusting of chocolate and vanilla from the barista—contents that now covered my dog.

Shadow was sniffing the ground and licking the pavement. She was on the scent and ready to track it back to the source. But I had the leash. I had control. She moved within striking distance of the cup and I fastened my grip.

She lurched for the cup and I felt a little pull. *No biggie,* I thought. I had the weight advantage and was low to the ground. Then she scrambled toward the cup with all her might. It was then that I realized my feet were facing the wrong direction. I'd lost mechanical advantage.

The leash rushed from my hand like a bull whip and vanished from my grasp. I fell to my knees, scraping them on the pavement, and pawed at the ground for anything leash-like. At last I had her, and reeled her in like a trout. She was panting and licking her snout. But she was back. I returned her to the tree trunk and I sat down on the ground. And I steamed.

That'll teach you, I said to myself, again.

I surveyed what remained of my drink. Three-quarters left in the cup and spillover on the pavement. I peered inside the café and saw that the customer line had grown several deep. Shadow nosed into me with a wet snout. We were together. A boy and his dog, the classic love story. So I reached for my coffee and drank.

That's the type of morning it was.

"Why, Peter, that's such a *beautiful drawing!*" a woman said.

A mom was talking with her son on a nearby bench. The little boy was around my daughter's age and was coloring with some crayons. The woman had a singsong voice that brimmed with cheer. You could almost hear her smile. She peered at her son's latest work.

"I didn't know the ocean was *that pretty!*" she said.

She had that upbeat, customer testimonial timbre I knew from infomercials for vegetable juicers and the Dootson School of Trucking. That was when Jobs's email popped up on my laptop.

"Holy fuck!" I yelled.

I looked around for someone to share in this good fortune, but found only a glare—hers. She stared at me, then turned back to her son.

"Peter, that must be the most fabulous shark *I've ever seen!*"

I hung my head in embarrassment and read. Jobs's thirteen-word response was short, but somehow this comforted me. Only the *real* Steve Jobs could've written *this*.

THE YEAR BEFORE iPHONE

I RECEIVED THE EMAIL FROM Jobs in 2006. This is a year that Apple watchers know well as The Year Before iPhone.

Jobs was riding high as the CEO of two behemoths: Apple and Pixar. Both companies had charged ahead on brazen new paths. Jobs was on the cover of *Time* that year with a headline that read, "The Man Who Always Seems to Know What's Next." Investors and the press couldn't get enough. The pressure on him had to have been intense.

But the tech world was in a trough without the iPhone. There were fewer startups focused on mobile technology. There was no Uber. No Tinder or Grindr. No Snapchat or Instagram. Twitter was only happening over SMS. Mobile apps were rudimentary artifices of the Blackberry at best.

I guess what I'm saying is that Jobs's worldview had shifted by 2006. The company had an idea for a revolutionary technology. An idea they hoped would bear fruit the following year.

A quick aside: Apple used to be known by another name—Apple *Computer*. The company name change happened in 2007, foreshadowing the move into smartphones, tablets, and digital media. Some of us old-timers actually remember when the company that now makes iPods, iPhones, and iPads only sold desktop computers.

Maybe Jobs's email to me was insignificant in the scheme of things. But it piqued my curiosity. Why did the billionaire bother to write me back?

Everything we knew about technology was about to change.

THE SECOND COMING

THE APPLE YOU KNOW TODAY is light years removed from Jobs's return to Cupertino. Today's Apple isn't just innovative. It's profitable. You probably hear the word "Apple" and think of its armada of shiny retail shops and sunny employees. You think of iPhones and iPads, iTunes and Apple TV.

But there was a darker time. A time when innovation at Apple was as rare as a Windows laptop on Jobs's desk. The year was 1997. In Jobs's speech at Macworld that year, he admitted as much, saying, "Apple is executing wonderfully on many of the wrong things." Apple board member and former Oracle CEO Larry Ellison concurred: "It's back to innovation."

This all happened just before I started working at Apple.

Jobs's 1997 arrival in Cupertino was heralded as the event of the year. *Time* called it his "triumphant return." Hosannas were heard from Infinite Loop to Wall Street. But Jobs rolled up to a very different Apple than the company he had co-founded in 1976.

Financial turmoil was Apple's companion in 1997. Apple was struggling in stagnation. *Forbes* said, "...demand for the Mac, its biggest moneymaker, was sinking, and the Cupertino, California-based company was on the brink of bankruptcy." Net profits were down and the company was vying for market share. As the Motley Fool said, "Morale was faltering...The place was in shambles."

But there was good news that year, too. Apple was entering into a partnership with Microsoft. A lawsuit between the two companies would be settled, and Internet Explorer would become the default browser on Macs. But that wasn't all.

Microsoft agreed to continue development of Microsoft Office for Macintosh. And Redmond put their money where their mouth was, agreeing to invest $150 million dollars in Apple. There was only one problem with this good news: its reception at Macworld.

Jobs is live on stage at Macworld 1997 and announces the new partnership to the crowd. He projects a slide onto the giant screen behind him that reads: MEANINGFUL PARTNERS. Then he tells the audience that he wants to introduce Apple's new partner and investor live via satellite.

That's when the face of Bill Gates pops up on the giant screen behind Jobs. Gates's live image is met by jeers and boos from the crowd. The Microsoft chairman stomachs the seconds-long audience pummeling and keeps his cool. He smiles and describes the value of the Microsoft-Apple partnership. He hits his talking points and finishes to a smattering of applause.

Later, in conversation with Walter Isaacson (featured in the biography *Steve Jobs*), Jobs called the Macworld announcement, "...my worst and stupidest staging mistake of my life." Seeing Gates on the giant screen may have even spooked some of the Apple faithful. "The scene," wrote Isaacson, "was such a brutal echo of Apple's famous 1984 Big Brother ad."

Macworld 1997 was supposed to be a day of good news. But to many, it was a day lost to the history between the two companies. *The Seattle Times* called the companies' relationship a "near-religious war." Rob Enderle, an analyst with Giga Information Group, said about Apple, "They've done everything they possibly could do to attack Microsoft, to disparage Microsoft." It was a conflict that would become ingrained in the Silicon Valley zeitgeist. Small versus Big. Good versus Evil. The Rebel Alliance versus the Evil Empire. It didn't matter that Gates had brought his checkbook to Macworld. Maybe the day was a *fait accompli*, a story written even before the two tech giants hit the stage.

The differences between Apple and Microsoft, the Macintosh and the PC, would be an ongoing theme in Apple's advertising. The dynamic would also play out almost ten years later in Apple's

2006 "Get a Mac" TV ad campaign. In fact, the campaign would play a role for me, too. The campaign is what spurred my email to Jobs in the first place. I had some concerns. And I would take them to the top.

ENTER THE FANBOY

I JOINED APPLE A YEAR after Jobs's return. I worked as a freelance communications manager in Apple Developer Connection (ADC). ADC was tasked with helping Apple developers build and deploy applications for the Mac.

Developers are the lifeblood of a computer company. They create the software and hardware that give your computers potential. *And they move units.*

You don't buy a Mac for its shiny patina. You buy a Mac for Photoshop or Dreamweaver. For Word or OmniGraffle. Developers transform your bricks of plastic, glass, metal, and circuit boards into tools. Apple knew what all computer makers know: Application sales drive hardware revenue.

The ADC website shows that the group provides SDKs (software development kits), software seeds (OS or operating system releases), developer support, news, and resources to developers. We also ran the yearly Worldwide Developers Conference (WWDC).

Technology evangelists were everywhere in ADC. Some of them were first-party (Apple) developers who worked onsite. These teams developed programs that ran exclusively on Macintosh— apps like iPhoto, Final Cut Pro, and iMovie. Third-party developers, on the other hand, worked offsite. They orbited Apple like satellites, but we made sure they were in contact with the home planet.

There were many days when I was tasked to write stories on Mac OS X technologies. Maybe I'd have to write a story about Mac OS X's graphical user interface. I'd call up one of our third-party developers and talk with them about their development. We'd discuss all things GUI, but our conversations were wide-ranging. We might touch on marketing or sales as well as development. I loved talking with our developers because it was like being at a cocktail party with the most interesting guests.

Jobs's talks were the backdrop to my time at Apple. He spoke to us at campus gatherings in Caffé Macs (the cafeteria) and the company auditorium. By the way, we called Jobs "S.J."— never "Jobs," "Steve," or "Mr. Jobs."

"S.J. believes this will be an important strategy," my coworker would say.

"S.J. is behind this one hundred percent," another would chime in.

"Why doesn't S.J.'s silver Mercedes have license plates? He passed me on 280 (a highway) last night and I didn't see any," I said. Nobody knew the answer.

My coworkers and I spent a lot of time in Caffé Macs. We'd hit the cafeteria for breakfast and lunch. Apple knew how to treat their employees, and the food was top-notch. Breakfasts were a particular hit; we'd wait in line and watch the short-order cooks whip up our meals. Pancakes and egg sandwiches were my favorites. One of my coworkers loved "crazy potatoes," a specialty of the house comprising fried potatoes plus eggs, cheese, salsa, and bacon or sausage.

My lunchtime staple was the tuna salad. But this was no mayonnaise-albacore concoction. It was a salad served with tender pieces of seared ahi on top that came with a side of wasabi dressing—and it was beyond delicious. I ate this for consecutive weeks. If you wanted panko-encrusted salmon with hoisin-ginger dressing, you could find that, too. There were rumors that Jobs had handpicked everything in the cafeteria himself. I never believed it. He had more pressing matters to attend to.

The café seating was casual. You'd just grab an open table, inside or out. The outside tables were great. On a sunny day, the patio outside Caffé Macs was packed. Nothing but sunshine, blue skies, and green grass. I noticed that some of the older programmers often sat together in the cafeteria. They'd hold court at this large circular table in the front by the entrance. Day after day, you'd see the same guys in the same spots. It was their usual lunchtime routine.

The auditorium seating was more formalized. As a freelancer, I wasn't given priority in the company auditorium during a Jobs speech. If there was an open seat after every employee had a chance to enter, then yes. But I didn't mind. I was free to stand outside and listen. In fact, my boss would often apologize to me for the exclusion. I wasn't bothered at all. I agreed: Employees first.

When it was sunny out at Caffé Macs, there was always the chance of a "celebrity sighting." I'd see Jonathan Ive having lunch with Jobs. Other times, Ive would dine with his cadre of designers or other employees.

The Apple designers were a breed apart. They were my favorite part of lunchtime. They looked just as you'd expect. Many had fun clothes, cool haircuts, and a sophisticated international vibe. I loved watching them. The skinny jeans, the logo T-shirts, and ubiquitous black clothing set them apart. Black was their favorite color. Of course.

The rest of us wore our work "uniforms," not that there was any sort of dress code that I remember. Most of the guys wore business casual. That meant button-down shirts and jeans or khakis. Women wore anything "California casual."

Deep inside, I was a fanboy. A loyalist. I'd been an Apple nut since the very beginning, so finding myself in Cupertino with Jobs at the helm was a real thrill. If I tried hard, I could remember the earlier me. The brace-faced teenager who'd once proposed buying an Apple to my parents. *It would be educational!* I said. I may have even believed it.

Our family ended up with an Apple][+, one of the first consumer products that the company sold. I thought I'd be able to cover the purchase with my bar mitzvah money, but I wasn't even close. It ended up costing around $2,000 for the 8-bit technological marvel with 64K of RAM, a monochrome screen, audio cassette storage, and three games. It had the computing power of a modern day children's toy, and I loved every nerdy minute of it.

All of this is to say that I was embraced by a supportive team in ADC. I even got the chance to work the booth at our annual developers' conference (WWDC), where I was able to talk to our developers in person. I grew to know our technology evangelists and our team in my short tenure there. One popular Apple technology book published at the time even thanked me personally in its pages. But that wasn't all.

This fanboy even got to play with one of the first iPods, before it was released to the public. I was living the dream.

NO, NO, NO, AND...

THE "GET A MAC" AD campaign is what did it. Apple's 2006 multi–million-dollar TV campaign was a smash. The TV spots ran and Mac sales spiked. More ads were produced and more Macs were sold. The campaign was a home run by any estimation.

But despite the campaign's popularity, I had mixed feelings about it. The TV spots were an odd combination of humor and smugness, starting off playful but quickly changing tack. They were the wrong tone, I thought. Arrogant. Disrespectful, even.

"Hello, I'm a Mac," the ads began. "And I'm a PC." I'm sure you remember the campaign. Apple's ad agency produced more than sixty spots in total. The U.S. ads featured actors John Hodgman as the "PC" and Justin Long as the

"Mac," positioning the two on opposite ends of the computer spectrum.

The spots would open up with a clever premise. This was the entry point to the computer problem. The attention getter. The witty repartee would move Hodgman and Long to the kicker. And the kicker was that "Mac" was a better choice. The series used sight gags, props, costumes, humor, and sarcasm to get its points across.

There were tons of PC facts and stereotypes to mine for the campaign, derived from the personal computer zeitgeist. The PC, as shown in the campaign, was clumsy, inelegant, harder to use, and more prone to crashes/viruses, device conflicts, etc. Hodgman's "PC" was also pasty-faced, middle-aged, uptight, bespectacled, and unstylish. Remind you of anyone?

The ads would pop up while I was watching primetime TV. They were creative, sure, but they also rubbed me the wrong way. So I asked my buddy, Jason, for Jobs's email address. And this is what I wrote to Jobs:

Mr. Jobs,

I'm sorry to trouble you, but I had a question about the new round of Apple "Get a Mac" ads.

1) Do you think the Bill Gates "character" might be offensive to Microsoft, especially given their generous $150 million dollar bailout of Apple in the 90s? Not to mention possibly disrespectful of their quality development of the ubiquitous Microsoft Office?

2) Do you think virus writers will now be chomping at the bit to write a virus to prove Apple's ad wrong?

3) Do you think that Apple's critics will view the Walt Mossberg plug as a way of influencing journalists that cover Apple?

4) Finally, do you think the Japanese "digital camera" woman is an offensive cultural stereotype?

Jobs's thirteen-word response?

1) No

2) They already are, but its (sic) much harder for OS X than Windows

3) No

4) No

Steve

And that was that. At least I had my moment in the sun, and he'd read what I'd sent him. But there was one more thing that happened while I worked at Apple: a chance encounter with to the most secretive part of the Cupertino campus.

POSTSCRIPT—

INTRUDER IN THE SECRET LAB

ESTABLISHING SHOT: DOWNTOWN CUPERTINO - NIGHT

We fade in on the glimmering city lights of Cupertino, California. We hold for a few beats, then pan down and left to reveal the rooftop of a modern high-rise.

EXT. HIGH-RISE ROOFTOP—NIGHT

Our HERO is alone on the roof of a building. He's dressed in all black and is wearing a backpack. He wears a climbing harness and his face is covered in greasepaint. We see he's handsome and fit. His hands work a device.

CUT TO: HERO'S HANDS

The HERO clips a metal cable into the carabineer on his vest. We hear a loud METALLIC CLICK.

BACK TO SCENE

We pull back to reveal a shiny HVAC unit on the roof. The HERO loops a giant metal climbing cable around the unit. We hear a METALLIC RUBBING SOUND as the cable tightens around its base. The HERO moves to the edge of the rooftop and looks out onto...

CLOSE-UP: HERO'S FACE

We look into his determined eyes.

Dramatic music BUILDS.

CUT TO: HERO'S POINT OF VIEW

We pan up slowly to reveal we're looking out onto the nighttime campus of...Apple.

Dramatic music SWELLS.

Several illuminated Apple logos shine in the darkness. There's no mistaking where we're at, or the challenge facing the HERO.

BACK TO SCENE

The HERO positions himself at the edge of the

rooftop. He pulls the climbing cable taut. He grips it in both hands and leans off the rooftop edge. He's dangling in midair, ten stories up, at a 45-degree angle to the ground. He's at the mercy of his equipment. We hear the GROAN of bending metal.

CLOSE UP: HERO'S FACE

We ZOOM in to the HERO. He turns and stares at the rooftop HVAC unit.

INSERT: HVAC UNIT

We PUSH-IN to reveal the HVAC metal supports bending under the weight of the HERO. We hear metal GROAN again.

BACK TO SCENE

Our HERO is already committed. He's hanging off the roof ledge, motionless in the darkness. He waits a few beats and shifts his weight. We hear a ROAR of stressed metal near its breaking point.

INSERT: HVAC UNIT

The rivets on the base of the HVAC are coming off the support column. We hear the POPPING of metal rivets as a few break loose.

BACK TO SCENE

The HERO looks down, licks his lips, and sets his jaw.

CUT TO: WIDE SHOT

The HERO leaps off the edge of the building into the darkness.

Music PUNCTUATES his leap and the dramatic descent. We cut between angles for effect as the

HERO rappels down the face of the building and swoops right past us.

• • •

ME? I'D LIKE HOLLYWOOD TO write a caper movie about the Apple Design Lab. I'd put our most creative minds to work on the story. It would include soaring highs and crushing setbacks. Moments of triumph and despair. Grief and grace. I'd love to watch a ragtag group of losers and misfits, arguing and double-crossing each other, trying to get in.

Hollywood could give the team some amazing tech to use in the heist. They would definitely outfit the lab with state-of-the-art countermeasures—I'm talking radical security features. Forget retinal scanners, voice-recognition, and facial biometrics. Me? I'd use red herrings if I were writing it.

I'd make it relatively easy to get into the lab (but not too easy). Then, I'd rig the place with devices that looked like cutting-edge Apple prototypes. These would be chrome and Lucite designs that were actually security triggers. You'd touch one of them and a locked cage would jettison from the ceiling, ensnaring you like a wild animal. *Blam!*

The folklore surrounding the Apple Design Lab is nearly as legendary as the place itself. These secret innovation labs always garner their share of nicknames. I've heard Apple's lab called their "skunkworks," the name that Lockheed Martin gave to their own innovation lab, which was wildly successful and became an incubator of many famous aircraft designs.

Theories abound on what makes a good skunkworks—a good idea incubator. But many businesses have adopted the Lockheed Martin paradigm: Set up a group of designers and engineers that is kept separate from the rest of your company. And remove the red tape. Get rid of the bureaucracy. *Give your designers the best toys and let them play.* Play and innovation are closely related. You can't have one without the other.

The idea behind these innovation labs is that autonomy begets creativity. Independence frees the mind. You hope to birth great things when you set up an innovation lab. But there are no rules. You kinda have to wing it.

You see, the Apple Design Lab is a members-only club. They don't do public tours and they don't do press. And they don't like uninvited guests.

I should know: I was one.

You may remember that I worked in ADC. My duties involved working with publishers and developers. This required a lot of contact with Apple employees.

I often needed to work directly with a specific employee who was the only one with access to the specific components we needed to keep a project moving. I might send this person an email request, but maybe I wouldn't hear back. I'd follow up with more emails, a phone call, voicemails. And, you guessed it: crickets.

My boss suggested another idea. Try a "drive-by" and see if these employees were at their desks. Find out if I could get them to respond to the personal touch. It was worth a shot.

I used the Apple Directory to divine the buildings where these people worked. For example, I'd find out that the guy I needed was in Building X, third floor, Office Y. He hadn't responded to me for weeks, so I'd walk over to Building X, touch my ID card to the sensor in the lobby, and head up to see him. It was easy. I'd find the guy and he'd apologize. He'd been out of town, on vacation, etc. He'd promise to get me what we needed, and we were done. This worked out great for a while.

I started doing these drive-bys routinely. I got comfortable with them. The employees I reached were generally nice. It was the same drill. Smile and state my purpose, then he or she would get me what I needed and I'd be on my way.

But then I found a different building. A different floor. The hallway was narrower. The lighting, dimmer. Even the ceiling was a little lower. Was it my perception, or were the walls closing in?

A man in front of me was walking fast, headed in my direction. I followed him as he swiped his badge and swung open a door. I "drafted" behind him into a spacious antechamber.

It was the security I noticed first. Men wearing black turtlenecks and aviator sunglasses stood at attention. There were at least four of them, two behind me and two in front. They stood in the corners wearing earpieces and dark suit jackets. Were they holding weapons? The scene looked like something you'd find at C.I.A. headquarters. There was loud music playing, too. A Euro beat. A club track. And there was a giant tiger caged in the corner. A tiger!

Two receptionists sat at a desk in front of me. A big sign behind them said, "THIS IS THE PLACE." This was it! I ran as fast as I could through the lobby and past security into the adjacent rooms. I looked around frantically for something valuable to grab. A souvenir. I spied a platinum-encrusted tech totem! I snatched it off the workbench and put it in my pocket, then turned and fled from the premises.

By the time I reached the quad, I could hear the helicopter coming. I was running fast and could hear voices yelling behind me. The whoop-whoop-whoop of the helicopter's blades washed over me as it landed in a cloud of dirt in front of Caffé Macs. I scrambled aboard and we rose into the sky.

"Bwhahahahahahaha!" I laughed as we soared into the air. I'd got what I wanted and just barely escaped.

Kidding. OK, seriously now, here's how it went down.

I'd followed the other employee into the new space—I was in. Inside the Apple Design Lab. Every fanboy's dream. The interior was white and I remember the lobby was sparse and modern like an upscale L.A. plastic surgery clinic. Everything was spotless.

A soft Euro beat was pulsing over the lobby speakers and two receptionists were sitting up front at a low desk. I asked one of the women for the person I was there to see.

"Who are you?" she asked.

"I'm looking for so-and-so," I repeated. I smiled.

"He doesn't work here," she said.

"Do you know where I can find him?" I asked.

"Who *are* you?" she asked.

"It's okay. Nevermind. Don't worry about it." I turned and headed out.

I left the building and was out on the Apple quad when I got that feeling you get when you think you're being followed. I turned around and found myself face to face with a burly security guard and a woman with a clipboard.

"Give me your ID badge," she said.

"Sure. Here you go."

I was relaxed and cooperative and didn't realize why everyone was so uptight. Of course, I didn't realize where I'd been until I got back to my desk. That's when it sunk in. And then I realized the gravity of the situation. I even went to my boss and explained what had happened.

"Don't worry about it. Thanks for telling me. It's no big deal," she said. And she was right.

Getting into the top-secret Apple Design Lab didn't require much after all. I didn't have to hack into a mainframe or defeat a retinal scan. I didn't have to match the timbre of Jonathan Ive's voice. I just walked through the front door.

But don't do what I did. They've added a lot more security since then.

They still remember when I got in.

ABOUT BRIAN BARTON

I always wanted to write. I wrote when I was younger to express myself and I do the exact same thing today. And I'm a big reader. Books, magazines, cereal boxes. Anything. My bookshelves are overflowing. Every project starts with research. I like to learn about a subject before I begin. I read, travel, and interview people and take notes on what I learn. I immerse myself in a topic because it's fun. Then, I write. This takes anywhere from months to years. When I'm done, I work with professional artists. They create book designs that I hope will capture your imagination. The result is writing steeped in real life. I hope you enjoy.

ACKNOWLEDGMENTS

Thanks to the family, friends, and colleagues who've been generous with support. Thank you, especially, to Bill, D.M.T., Emily, J.Y, Jeffy, Julia, Kiran, and Sandeep.

THANK YOU

Thanks for your emails, tweets, comments, and questions. Word of mouth is essential for self-published authors like me. Please write a review on Amazon or Goodreads if you can. Thanks.

—*B.B.*
New York City